C++ MADE EASY

A BEGINNER'S GUIDE TO PROGRAMMING POWER

OLIVER LUCAS JR

TABLE OF CONTENTS

Chapter 7

Chapter 8

Chapter 9

Chapter 10

Preface

Welcome to "C++ Made Easy: A Beginner's Guide to Programming Power"! This book is your passport to the exciting world of C++ programming. Whether you're a complete novice or have some coding experience, this book will guide you through the fundamentals and beyond, empowering you to create your own amazing programs.

C++ is a powerful and versatile language that's used in everything from game development and operating systems to scientific research and high-performance computing. It's a language that can open doors to a wide range of career opportunities and enable you to build almost anything you can imagine.

But learning C++ can be daunting, especially for beginners. That's why this book is designed with clarity and simplicity in mind. We'll break down complex concepts into bite-sized pieces, using clear explanations, practical examples, and engaging exercises to make your learning journey enjoyable and rewarding.

What You'll Learn

In this book, you'll discover:

The core elements of C++, including variables, data types, operators, and control flow.

How to write functions to organize and reuse your code.

The power of object-oriented programming with classes, objects, inheritance, and polymorphism.

How to work with arrays and strings to process collections of data.

The essentials of memory management, including pointers, dynamic memory allocation, and preventing memory leaks.

Techniques for file handling, reading and writing data to files.

Advanced concepts like templates and the Standard Template Library (STL).

How to apply your knowledge by building your first C++ project.

Who This Book Is For

This book is perfect for:

Absolute beginners with no prior programming experience.

Students learning C++ in a classroom setting.

Hobbyists who want to explore the world of programming.

Professionals from other fields who want to add C++ to their skillset.

How to Use This Book

This book is designed to be read sequentially, as each chapter builds upon the concepts introduced in previous chapters. However, you can also use it as a reference guide, jumping to specific sections as needed.

We encourage you to actively engage with the material by working through the examples and exercises. Don't be afraid to experiment and try things out. The best way to learn C++ is by writing code!

Our Goal

Our goal is to make learning C++ accessible and enjoyable for everyone. We believe that anyone can learn to code, and we're here to guide you on your journey. We hope this book empowers you to unlock your coding potential and create amazing things with C++.

So, let's get started! Open your IDE, fire up your compiler, and get ready to dive into the world of C++ programming.

Chapter 1

Welcome to the World of C++

1.1 Why C++? (Power, versatility, career opportunities)

Why C++?

So, you're thinking about learning to code. Awesome! But why choose C++? In a world overflowing with programming languages, C++ stands out as a true powerhouse. It's like the Swiss Army knife of coding – versatile, reliable, and capable of tackling almost any task you throw at it.

Unleash the Power

C++ is renowned for its raw speed and efficiency. When milliseconds matter – think high-speed trading, game development, or cutting-edge scientific simulations – C++ delivers the performance you need. It gives you fine-grained control over your computer's hardware and memory, allowing you to squeeze every ounce of performance out of your machine.

Think of it like this: if programming languages were cars, C++ would be a finely-tuned sports car. It might require a bit more skill to handle, but the payoff is incredible speed and responsiveness.

Versatility at its Core

From building operating systems that power millions of devices to creating breathtaking video games that transport you to other worlds, C++ is everywhere. Its flexibility is unmatched. Whether you're interested in artificial intelligence, robotics, finance, or web development, C++ has the tools you need to bring your ideas to life.

And with its support for different programming styles – procedural, object-oriented, and generic – C++ adapts to your needs, not the other way around. This versatility makes it a language that can grow with you as your skills and ambitions evolve.

A World of Opportunities

Learning C++ isn't just about mastering a powerful language; it's about unlocking a world of career opportunities. Skilled C++ developers are in high demand across a wide range of industries.

Imagine yourself:

Designing the next generation of video games that captivate millions.

Developing cutting-edge software that revolutionizes healthcare or finance.

Building the systems that power self-driving cars or explore the depths of space.

With C++, the possibilities are endless. It's a language that can take you anywhere you want to go.

Ready to embark on this exciting journey? Let's dive in!

1.2 Setting Up Your Coding Environment

Okay, you're fired up about C++ – awesome! Now, let's get your computer ready to code. Think of this as setting up your workshop. You need the right tools before you can start building amazing things.

Choosing Your Compiler

First things first, you need a **compiler**. This is a special program that takes your human-readable C++ code and translates it into instructions your computer can understand. It's like a magical translator for your computer!

There are a few popular options out there:

g++ (GNU Compiler Collection): A powerful and widely-used compiler that's free and open-source. It's available for most operating systems.

Clang: Another excellent free and open-source compiler known for its helpful error messages and fast compile times.

Microsoft Visual C++: If you're using Windows, this compiler comes bundled with Visual Studio, a popular Integrated Development Environment (more on that below!).

Don't worry too much about the differences between these compilers for now. They all do essentially the same thing. We'll provide clear instructions on how to install your chosen compiler later in this chapter.

Integrated Development Environments (IDEs)

Next up, you'll want an **Integrated Development Environment (IDE)**. This is like a super-powered text editor with built-in tools specifically designed for coding. IDEs make writing, organizing, and debugging your code much easier.

Here are a few popular choices:

Code::Blocks: A free, open-source, and cross-platform IDE that's great for beginners. It's lightweight and easy to use.

Visual Studio: A powerful IDE from Microsoft, packed with features. It's a great choice if you're using Windows.

Xcode: If you're on a Mac, Xcode is Apple's official IDE, and it's free and easy to use.

CLion: A cross-platform IDE from JetBrains with advanced features like smart code completion and refactoring tools.

Again, the best IDE for you depends on your personal preferences and operating system. We'll guide you through setting up a popular IDE later in the chapter.

Your First C++ Program

Now for the fun part! Let's write your very first C++ program. It's a tradition among programmers to start with a program that prints "Hello, world!" to the screen.

Here's the code:

```cpp
C++

#include <iostream>

int main() {
  std::cout << "Hello, world!" << std::endl;
  return 0;
}
```

Don't worry if this looks like gibberish right now. We'll explain everything in detail soon. For now, just type this code into your chosen IDE and run it. If everything is set up correctly, you should see "Hello, world!" printed on your screen.

1.3 Basic Building Blocks: Variables, Data Types, and Input/Output

Alright, let's get down to the nuts and bolts of C++ programming! In this section, we'll explore the fundamental building blocks that make up every C++ program: variables, data types, and input/output.

Variables: Storing Information

Imagine variables as containers that hold information in your program. They're like little boxes where you can store numbers, text, or other kinds of data.

To use a variable, you need to give it a name and tell C++ what type of data it will hold. Here's how:

C++

```
int age = 25;        // An integer variable named
"age" storing the value 25
double price = 9.99; // A floating-point variable
named "price" storing 9.99
char initial = 'J';   // A character variable
named "initial" storing the letter 'J'
```

Think of the variable's name as a label on the box, and the data type as the kind of things you can put inside the box.

Data Types: What Kind of Information?

C++ offers a variety of data types to store different kinds of information:

`int`: For storing whole numbers (integers) like 10, -5, or 1000.

`double`: For storing numbers with decimal points (floating-point numbers) like 3.14, -2.5, or 0.001.

`char`: For storing single characters like 'A', '?', or '$'.

`bool`: For storing truth values, either `true` or `false`.

`string`: For storing sequences of characters (text) like "Hello, world!".

Choosing the right data type is important because it tells C++ how to interpret and work with the data you store in your variables.

Input/Output: Interacting with the User

A program isn't very useful if it can't communicate with the outside world! That's where input and output come in.

Input: This is how your program receives information from the user or other sources. In C++, we often use `cin` (pronounced "see-in") to get input from the keyboard.

C++

```
int age;
std::cout << "Enter your age: ";
std::cin >> age;
```

Output: This is how your program displays information to the user. We use `cout` (pronounced "see-out") to print things to the console.

C++

```
std::cout << "Your age is: " << age << std::endl;
```

The `std::endl` adds a newline character, moving the cursor to the next line for subsequent output.

Putting it Together

Let's combine these concepts in a simple example:

C++

```
#include <iostream>
#include <string>

int main() {
    std::string name;
    int age;

    std::cout << "Enter your name: ";
    std::cin >> name;

    std::cout << "Enter your age: ";
    std::cin >> age;

    std::cout << "Hello, " << name << "! You are "
<< age << " years old." << std::endl;
```

```
    return 0;
}
```

This program asks the user for their name and age, stores them in variables, and then prints a personalized greeting.

Chapter 2

Controlling the Flow

2.1 Making Decisions with `if` and `else`

Up until now, our programs have executed code line by line, from top to bottom. But what if you want your program to make decisions and execute different code blocks based on certain conditions? That's where `if` and `else` come in!

The `if` Statement

The `if` statement allows you to execute a block of code only if a specific condition is true. It's like saying, "If this is true, then do this."

Here's the basic syntax:

C++

```cpp
if (condition) {
  // Code to execute if the condition is true
}
```

The `condition` is an expression that evaluates to either `true` or `false`. If the condition is `true`, the code inside the curly braces `{}` is executed. Otherwise, the code block is skipped.

Example:

C++

```cpp
int age = 18;
```

```cpp
if (age >= 18) {
    std::cout << "You are eligible to vote!" <<
std::endl;
}
```

In this example, the code will print "You are eligible to vote!" because the condition `age >= 18` is true.

The `else` Statement

The `else` statement provides an alternative code block to execute if the `if` condition is false. It's like saying, "If this is true, then do this; otherwise, do that."

Here's the syntax:

C++

```cpp
if (condition) {
  // Code to execute if the condition is true
} else {
  // Code to execute if the condition is false
}
```

Example:

Code snippet

```cpp
int age = 15;

if (age >= 18) {
    std::cout << "You are eligible to vote!" <<
std::endl;
```

```cpp
} else {
    std::cout << "You are not yet eligible to
vote." << std::endl;
}
```

In this case, the code will print "You are not yet eligible to vote." because the condition `age >= 18` is false.

Logical Operators

Logical operators allow you to combine multiple conditions in your `if` statements:

`&&` **(AND)**: Both conditions must be true for the overall expression to be true.

C++

```cpp
if (age >= 18 && hasLicense == true) {
    std::cout << "You can drive!" << std::endl;
}
```

`||` **(OR)**: At least one of the conditions must be true for the overall expression to be true.

C++

```cpp
if (isWeekend == true || isHoliday == true) {
    std::cout << "Time to relax!" << std::endl;
}
```

! **(NOT):** Reverses the truth value of a condition.

C++

```cpp
if (!isRaining) {
    std::cout << "Let's go for a walk!" <<
std::endl;
}
```

Nesting `if` **and** `else`

You can also nest `if` and `else` statements to create more complex decision-making logic.

C++

```cpp
if (temperature > 30) {
  std::cout << "It's hot outside!" << std::endl;
} else {
  if (temperature < 10) {
        std::cout << "It's cold outside!" <<
std::endl;
  } else {
     std::cout << "The weather is pleasant." <<
std::endl;
  }
}
```

Making Your Code More Readable

Use indentation to clearly show which code belongs to which block.

Use meaningful variable names to make your code easier to understand.

Add comments to explain complex logic or conditions.

With `if` and `else`, you can create programs that respond intelligently to different situations. In the next section, we'll learn about loops, which allow you to repeat code blocks multiple times.

2.2 Repeating Actions with Loops (`for`, `while`, `do-while`)

Imagine you need to print "Hello, world!" ten times. Would you write the same `cout` statement ten times? That's where loops come in handy! Loops allow you to repeat a block of code multiple times, making your programs more efficient and powerful.

C++ offers three main types of loops: `for`, `while`, and `do-while`. Let's explore each one.

The `for` Loop

The `for` loop is perfect when you know exactly how many times you want to repeat a code block. It's like saying, "Do this 10 times" or "Do this for each item in a list."

Here's the basic syntax:

C++

```cpp
for (initialization; condition; update) {
  // Code to execute repeatedly
}
```

Initialization: This happens only once at the beginning of the loop. You usually declare a counter variable here.

Condition: This is checked before each iteration. If it's true, the loop continues; otherwise, it stops.

Update: This happens after each iteration. You usually increment or decrement the counter variable here.

Example:

C++

```
for (int i = 0; i < 10; i++) {
  std::cout << "Hello, world! (" << i + 1 << ")"
<< std::endl;
}
```

This code will print "Hello, world! (1)" through "Hello, world! (10)".

The `while` **Loop**

The `while` loop is used when you want to repeat a code block as long as a certain condition is true. It's like saying, "Keep doing this while this is true."

Here's the syntax:

C++

```
while (condition) {
  // Code to execute repeatedly
}
```

The condition is checked before each iteration. If it's true, the loop continues; otherwise, it stops.

Example:

C++

```
int number = 1;

while (number <= 5) {
   std::cout << number << " ";
   number++;
}
```

This code will print "1 2 3 4 5 ".

The do-while **Loop**

The do-while loop is similar to the while loop, but it guarantees that the code block is executed at least once, even if the condition is initially false. It's like saying, "Do this at least once, and then keep doing it while this is true."

Here's the syntax:

C++

```
do {
   // Code to execute repeatedly
} while (condition);
```

The condition is checked after each iteration. If it's true, the loop continues; otherwise, it stops.

Example:

C++

```
int number = 6; // Condition is false initially

do {
  std::cout << number << " ";
  number++;
} while (number <= 5);
```

This code will print "6 " even though the condition `number <= 5` is false from the start.

Choosing the Right Loop

Use `for` when you know the exact number of iterations.

Use `while` when you want to loop as long as a condition is true.

Use `do-while` when you need to execute the code block at least once.

Important Notes:

Be careful to avoid infinite loops! Make sure your loop condition eventually becomes false.

Use meaningful variable names for your loop counters.

Add comments to explain complex loop logic.

With loops, you can automate repetitive tasks and create more dynamic and interesting programs. In the next section, we'll dive into functions, which allow you to organize your code into reusable blocks.

2.3 Jumping Around with `switch` and `break`

Sometimes you need to choose between multiple options, like a choose-your-own-adventure book for your code. While you could use a series of `if` and `else` `if` statements, the `switch` statement provides a cleaner and more efficient way to handle multi-way branching.

The `switch` Statement

The `switch` statement evaluates an expression and jumps to the corresponding `case` label that matches the expression's value. It's like saying, "Check this value, and then jump to the matching section."

Here's the basic syntax:

C++

```cpp
switch (expression) {
  case value1:
    // Code to execute if expression == value1
    break;
  case value2:
    // Code to execute if expression == value2
    break;
  // ... more cases
  default:
    // Code to execute if no case matches
}
```

`expression`: The value to be compared against the case labels.

`case value:`: A label that specifies a possible value for the expression.

`break;`: A statement that exits the `switch` block.

`default:`: An optional label that catches any values not covered by the other cases.

Example:

C++

```
int day = 3;

switch (day) {
  case 1:
    std::cout << "Monday" << std::endl;
    break;
  case 2:
    std::cout << "Tuesday" << std::endl;
    break;
  case 3:
    std::cout << "Wednesday" << std::endl;
    break;
  // ... more cases
  default:
        std::cout << "Invalid day number" << std::endl;
}
```

This code will print "Wednesday" because the value of `day` is 3.

The Importance of `break`

The `break` statement is crucial in a `switch` statement. Without it, the code would "fall through" to the next case, potentially executing unintended code.

Example (without `break`**):**

C++

```cpp
int day = 2;

switch (day) {
  case 1:
    std::cout << "Monday" << std::endl;
  case 2:
    std::cout << "Tuesday" << std::endl;
  case 3:
    std::cout << "Wednesday" << std::endl;
  default:
        std::cout  <<  "Invalid  day  number"  <<
std::endl;
}
```

This code would print:

```
Tuesday
Wednesday
Invalid day number
```

This is because there are no `break` statements to stop the execution flow.

When to Use `switch`

When you have multiple possible values to compare against.

When the comparisons involve equality (`==`) rather than more complex conditions.

When you want to make your code more readable and organized.

Important Notes:

The `case` labels must be constant integral values (e.g., integers, characters).

The `default` case is optional but recommended for handling unexpected values.

With `switch` and `break`, you can create efficient and readable code for handling multiple choices. In the next section, we'll delve into functions, a powerful tool for organizing and reusing your code.

Chapter 3

Functions: Building Blocks of Code

3.1 What is a Function?

Imagine you're building with LEGOs. Instead of sticking individual bricks together every time you need a window or a door, you could create reusable modules for these common elements. Functions in C++ are like those LEGO modules – they're self-contained blocks of code that perform specific tasks.

Defining a Function

Here's the basic structure of a function in C++:

C++

```
return_type function_name(parameter_list) {
  // Code to be executed (function body)
  return value; // (Optional)
}
```

`return_type`: The type of data the function returns (e.g., `int`, `double`, `void` if it doesn't return anything).

`function_name`: A descriptive name for your function (e.g., `calculateArea`, `printGreeting`).

`parameter_list`: A comma-separated list of input values (parameters) the function accepts (e.g., `int length, int width`).

`function body`: The code that performs the function's task.

`return value`: The value the function sends back to the caller (if applicable).

Example:

C++

```cpp
int addNumbers(int a, int b) {
  int sum = a + b;
  return sum;
}
```

This function, named `addNumbers`, takes two integers (`a` and `b`) as input, calculates their sum, and returns the result.

Calling a Function

To use a function, you "call" it by its name and provide any required input values (arguments).

C++

```cpp
int result = addNumbers(5, 3); // result will
store 8
```

Modularity: Organizing Your Code

Functions help you break down complex programs into smaller, more manageable pieces. This modularity makes your code:

Easier to understand: Each function focuses on a specific task, making the overall logic clearer.

Easier to debug: If there's an error, you can isolate it to a specific function.

Easier to maintain: Changes to one function are less likely to affect other parts of your code.

Reusability: Write Once, Use Many Times

Once you've defined a function, you can call it multiple times from different parts of your program. This reusability:

Saves time and effort: You don't have to rewrite the same code repeatedly.

Reduces errors: You only need to test and debug the function once.

Improves consistency: The function will always perform the same task in the same way.

Example:

C++

```cpp
int main() {
  int result1 = addNumbers(10, 5);
  int result2 = addNumbers(7, 2);

    std::cout << "Result 1: " << result1 <<
std::endl; // Output: Result 1: 15
    std::cout << "Result 2: " << result2 <<
std::endl; // Output: Result 2: 9

  return 0;
}
```

In this example, the `addNumbers` function is called twice with different arguments, demonstrating its reusability.

By using functions effectively, you can write cleaner, more organized, and more efficient C++ code. In the next section, we'll explore different ways to define and use functions, including function overloading and default parameters.

3.2 Defining and Calling Functions: Parameters, Arguments, and Return Values

Let's dive deeper into the mechanics of functions and how to use them effectively in your C++ programs.

Parameters: The Function's Input

Think of parameters as placeholders for values that you'll provide to the function when you call it. They act like variables within the function's code block.

When defining a function, you specify the parameters within the parentheses after the function name:

C++

```cpp
int calculateArea(int length, int width) {   // length and width are parameters
  // ... function body
}
```

In this example, `calculateArea` expects two integer values: `length` and `width`.

Arguments: The Actual Values

When you call a function, you provide the actual values for the parameters. These values are called arguments.

C++

```cpp
int area = calculateArea(5, 10); // 5 and 10 are
arguments
```

Here, 5 is passed as the argument for `length`, and 10 is passed as the argument for `width`.

Matching Parameters and Arguments

C++ matches arguments to parameters based on their order. The first argument is assigned to the first parameter, the second argument to the second parameter, and so on. It's important to ensure that the number and types of arguments match the function's definition.

Return Values: The Function's Output

A function can optionally return a value back to the caller. This is done using the `return` statement.

C++

```cpp
int calculateArea(int length, int width) {
  int area = length * width;
  return area; // Returns the calculated area
}
```

The `return` statement does two things:

1 Ends the function's execution: Control immediately returns to the caller.

2 Sends a value back to the caller: The value after `return` is sent back to where the function was called.

The `void` Return Type

If a function doesn't need to return a value, you use the `void` return type.

C++

```cpp
void printGreeting(std::string name) {
    std::cout << "Hello, " << name << "!" << std::endl;
  // No return statement needed
}
```

Using Return Values

The return value of a function can be:

Stored in a variable:

C++

```cpp
int area = calculateArea(5, 10);
```

Used in an expression:

C++

```cpp
std::cout << "The area is: " << calculateArea(5, 10) << std::endl;
```

Passed as an argument to another function:

C++

```cpp
int   volume   =   calculateVolume(calculateArea(5,
10), 3);
```

Example: Putting it All Together

C++

```cpp
#include <iostream>

double calculateCircleArea(double radius) {
    const double PI = 3.14159;
    double area = PI * radius * radius;
    return area;
}

int main() {
    double radius;

    std::cout << "Enter the radius of the circle:
";
    std::cin >> radius;

    double area = calculateCircleArea(radius);

    std::cout << "The area of the circle is: " <<
area << std::endl;

    return 0;
}
```

This program defines a function `calculateCircleArea` that takes the radius as input and returns the calculated area. The `main` function gets the radius from the user, calls `calculateCircleArea`, and prints the result.

By understanding parameters, arguments, and return values, you can effectively define and use functions to create modular and reusable code in your C++ programs.

3.3 Function Overloading: Flexibility and Code Organization

In C++, you can have multiple functions with the same name, as long as they have different parameters. This is called **function overloading**. It's like having different tools with the same name but designed for different purposes – like a set of screwdrivers with different head types.

How Does it Work?

The compiler determines which version of the overloaded function to call based on the arguments you provide. It looks at the number of arguments and their data types to find the best match.

Example:

C++

```cpp
int add(int a, int b) {
  return a + b;
}

double add(double a, double b) {
  return a + b;
}
```

```cpp
int main() {
  int sum1 = add(5, 3);      // Calls the integer
version (returns 8)
    double sum2 = add(2.5, 7.1); // Calls the
double version (returns 9.6)
  return 0;
}
```

In this example, we have two functions named add. One takes two integers and returns an integer, while the other takes two doubles and returns a double. When you call add(5, 3), the compiler knows to use the integer version because the arguments are integers.

Benefits of Function Overloading

Flexibility: You can use the same function name for operations that perform similar tasks but with different data types. This makes your code more intuitive and easier to use.

Code Organization: Overloading helps group related functions together, improving the structure and readability of your code.

Reduced Naming Conflicts: You don't have to come up with different names for functions that essentially do the same thing (e.g., addInts, addDoubles).

Example: A More Realistic Scenario

Imagine you're writing a program to calculate the area of different shapes. You could overload a function named calculateArea:

C++

```cpp
int calculateArea(int length, int width) {   //
Area of a rectangle
```

```
    return length * width;
}

double calculateArea(double radius) {          //
Area of a circle
    const double PI = 3.14159;
    return PI * radius * radius;
}

double calculateArea(double base, double height)
{ // Area of a triangle
    return 0.5 * base * height;
}
```

Now you can use `calculateArea` for rectangles, circles, and triangles, making your code more consistent and user-friendly.

Important Notes

You cannot overload functions based on the return type alone. The compiler needs to be able to distinguish between overloaded functions based on their parameters.

Overloading can sometimes make it harder to understand which version of the function is being called. Use clear parameter names and comments to avoid confusion.

Function overloading is a powerful tool for writing flexible and well-organized C++ code. By understanding how it works, you can create more intuitive and maintainable programs.

Chapter 4

Working with Data

4.1 Arrays: Organizing Collections

Imagine you need to store the names of all the students in a class. Would you create a separate variable for each student? That would quickly become messy and difficult to manage. Arrays provide a solution by allowing you to store a collection of values of the same data type under a single name.

Declaring an Array

To declare an array, you specify the data type, followed by the array name and the number of elements it will hold within square brackets [].

C++

```
int scores[5];  // An array named "scores" that
can hold 5 integers
double prices[10]; // An array named "prices"
that can hold 10 doubles
char letters[26]; // An array named "letters"
that can hold 26 characters
```

This creates space in memory to store the specified number of elements.

Accessing Array Elements

You can access individual elements in an array using their **index**. The index starts from 0 for the first element and goes up to (size - 1) for the last element.

C++

```cpp
scores[0] = 95;   // Assign 95 to the first
element
scores[1] = 80;   // Assign 80 to the second
element
// ... and so on

std::cout << scores[3]; // Print the value of the
fourth element
```

Initializing an Array

You can initialize an array with values when you declare it:

C++

```cpp
int ages[3] = {25, 30, 28};
```

Or you can initialize it later, element by element:

C++

```cpp
std::string names[2];
names[0] = "Alice";
names[1] = "Bob";
```

Manipulating Arrays

You can use loops to efficiently process array elements:

C++

```cpp
int numbers[5] = {1, 2, 3, 4, 5};

for (int i = 0; i < 5; i++) {
   std::cout << numbers[i] * 2 << " "; // Print
each number multiplied by 2
}
```

This code will print: 2 4 6 8 10

Example: Finding the Average Score

C++

```cpp
#include <iostream>

int main() {
   int scores[5] = {85, 90, 78, 95, 88};
   int sum = 0;

   for (int i = 0; i < 5; i++) {
     sum += scores[i];
   }

   double average = static_cast<double>(sum) / 5;

   std::cout << "The average score is: " <<
average << std::endl;

   return 0;
```

```
}
```

This program calculates the average of five scores stored in an array.

Important Notes

Bounds Checking: Be careful not to access elements outside the bounds of the array (e.g., `scores[5]` in the example above). This can lead to unexpected behavior or program crashes.

Array Size: The size of an array is fixed once it's declared. You cannot change the size of an array later in the program.

Arrays are a fundamental data structure in C++ that allow you to efficiently organize and manipulate collections of data. By understanding how to declare, access, and manipulate arrays, you can write more powerful and versatile programs.

4.2 Strings: Textual Data

While individual characters (`char`) are useful for storing single letters or symbols, you often need to work with sequences of characters, like words, sentences, or entire paragraphs. That's where strings come in!

Character Arrays: The Old School Way

In C++, you can represent strings as arrays of characters. Remember that a character array needs an extra space for a special null character (`\0`) that marks the end of the string.

C++

```cpp
char greeting[7] = "Hello";  // {'H', 'e', 'l',
'l', 'o', '\0'}
```

This creates an array named `greeting` that stores the characters 'H', 'e', 'l', 'l', 'o', and the null terminator `\0`.

String Objects: The Modern Approach

C++ also provides a more convenient way to work with strings using the `std::string` class (you'll need to `#include` `<string>` at the top of your file). String objects are more flexible and offer a wide range of built-in functions for manipulating strings.

C++

```
#include <string>

std::string message = "Hello, world!";
```

This creates a string object named `message` that holds the text "Hello, world!".

String Manipulation

Both character arrays and string objects allow you to manipulate textual data. Here are some common operations:

Concatenation: Joining strings together.

C++

```
std::string firstName = "John";
std::string lastName = "Doe";
std::string  fullName  =  firstName  +  "  "  +
lastName; // fullName is "John Doe"
```

Length: Finding the number of characters in a string.

C++

```cpp
std::string text = "Coding is fun!";
int length = text.length(); // length is 14
```

Access individual characters:

C++

```cpp
std::string word = "Example";
char firstLetter = word[0]; // firstLetter is 'E'
```

Comparison: Checking if two strings are equal.

C++

```cpp
std::string str1 = "apple";
std::string str2 = "banana";
if (str1 == str2) {
    // ...
} else {
    // ...
}
```

Substrings: Extracting a portion of a string.

C++

```cpp
std::string text = "Programming";
std::string sub = text.substr(3, 4); // sub is
"gram" (starts at index 3, length 4)
```

Advantages of std::string

Dynamic Size: String objects can grow or shrink as needed, unlike fixed-size character arrays.

Memory Management: String objects handle memory allocation and deallocation automatically.

Rich Functionality: The std::string class provides many built-in functions for common string operations (e.g., searching, replacing, converting case).

Example: Analyzing a Sentence

C++

```cpp
#include <iostream>
#include <string>

int main() {
  std::string sentence;

  std::cout << "Enter a sentence: ";
```

```cpp
    std::getline(std::cin, sentence); // Read the
whole line, including spaces

    int numWords = 1; // Start with 1 to account
for the first word
    for (int i = 0; i < sentence.length(); i++) {
        if (sentence[i] == ' ') {
            numWords++;
        }
    }

    std::cout << "The sentence has " << numWords <<
" words." << std::endl;

    return 0;
}
```

This program reads a sentence from the user and counts the number of words by looking for spaces.

By understanding how to work with strings, you can process and manipulate textual data effectively in your C++ programs. The `std::string` class provides a powerful and convenient way to handle strings, making your code cleaner and more efficient.

4.3 Structures: Grouping Related Data

Imagine you're creating a program to manage a library catalog. You need to store information about each book, such as its title, author, ISBN, and publication year. Instead of creating separate variables for each piece of information, you can use structures to group this related data together.

What are Structures?

Structures are user-defined data types that allow you to combine different data types into a single unit. They're like blueprints for creating complex variables that hold multiple pieces of related information.

Defining a Structure

You define a structure using the `struct` keyword, followed by the structure name and a list of its members (variables) within curly braces `{}`.

C++

```cpp
struct Book {
  std::string title;
  std::string author;
  int year;
  long long isbn;
};
```

This defines a structure named `Book` with four members: `title`, `author`, `year`, and `isbn`.

Creating Structure Variables

Once you've defined a structure, you can create variables of that type:

C++

```cpp
Book book1;  // Create a variable named "book1"
of type "Book"
```

Accessing Members

You can access the members of a structure variable using the dot operator (.).

C++

```cpp
book1.title = "The Lord of the Rings";
book1.author = "J.R.R. Tolkien";
book1.year = 1954;
book1.isbn = 9780618002213;

std::cout << "Title: " << book1.title << std::endl;
```

Why Use Structures?

Organization: Structures help organize your data by grouping related information together.

Readability: They make your code more readable and easier to understand by giving meaningful names to groups of data.

Modularity: Structures can be passed as arguments to functions and returned from functions, promoting code reusability.

Example: A Simple Address Book

C++

```cpp
#include <iostream>
#include <string>

struct Contact {
  std::string name;
  std::string phoneNumber;
  std::string email;
```

```cpp
};

int main() {
  Contact contact1;

  std::cout << "Enter contact name: ";
  std::getline(std::cin, contact1.name);

  std::cout << "Enter phone number: ";
  std::getline(std::cin, contact1.phoneNumber);

  std::cout << "Enter email address: ";
  std::getline(std::cin, contact1.email);

  std::cout << "\nContact Information:\n";
  std::cout << "Name: " << contact1.name << std::endl;
  std::cout << "Phone: " << contact1.phoneNumber << std::endl;
  std::cout << "Email: " << contact1.email << std::endl;

  return 0;
}
```

This program defines a `Contact` structure to store name, phone number, and email. It then creates a `Contact` variable, gets the contact information from the user, and prints it.

By using structures, you can create more complex and organized data representations in your C++ programs. They are a powerful tool for managing related information and improving the clarity of your code.

Chapter 5

Pointers: The Key to Efficiency

5.1 Understanding Memory Addresses

Imagine your computer's memory as a vast city with many houses (memory locations). Each house has a unique address, and each house can store something different (data).

Variables and Memory Addresses

When you declare a variable in C++, the computer assigns it a specific memory address where its value is stored. Think of it as your variable having its own house in the city of memory.

C++

```
int age = 25;
```

This creates an integer variable named `age` and stores the value 25 at its assigned memory address.

Pointers: Holding Memory Addresses

A pointer is a special type of variable that holds the memory address of another variable. It's like having a piece of paper with the address of your variable's house written on it.

To declare a pointer, you use the asterisk (*) before the variable name:

C++

```
int *ptr;   // Declares a pointer named "ptr" that
can hold the address of an integer variable
```

The Address-of Operator (&)

To get the memory address of a variable, you use the address-of operator (&):

C++

```
int age = 25;

ptr = &age;    //   "ptr" now holds the memory
address of "age"
```

Now, `ptr` points to the memory location where the value of `age` is stored.

Dereferencing: Accessing the Value

To access the value stored at the memory address held by a pointer, you use the dereference operator (*):

C++

```
int value = *ptr; //   "value" now holds 25 (the
value stored at the address pointed to by "ptr")
```

Think of dereferencing as going to the house whose address is written on your piece of paper (`ptr`) and seeing what's inside (the value of `age`).

Why Use Pointers?

Direct Memory Access: Pointers allow you to directly access and manipulate data in memory. This can be more efficient than working with copies of data.

Dynamic Memory Allocation: Pointers are essential for working with dynamically allocated memory (memory that is allocated during program execution).

Passing Data by Reference: Pointers enable you to pass data to functions by reference, allowing the function to modify the original data.

Example: Swapping Values

C++

```cpp
#include <iostream>


void swap(int *a, int *b) {

  int temp = *a;

  *a = *b;

  *b = temp;

}


int main() {

  int x = 10;

  int y = 20;
```

```cpp
    std::cout << "Before swap: x = " << x << ", y =
" << y << std::endl;


    swap(&x, &y); // Pass the addresses of x and y


    std::cout << "After swap: x = " << x << ", y =
" << y << std::endl;


    return 0;

}
```

This program demonstrates how pointers can be used to swap the values of two variables. The `swap` function takes pointers to the variables, allowing it to modify the original values.

Understanding memory addresses and pointers is crucial for writing efficient and powerful C++ programs. While they might seem a bit complex at first, with practice, you'll be able to wield these tools effectively.

5.2 Pointer Arithmetic and Arrays

Pointers and arrays have a close relationship in C++. In fact, array names can often be treated as pointers, which opens up powerful ways to work with arrays using pointer arithmetic.

Arrays as Pointers

When you declare an array, the array name itself acts as a pointer to the first element of the array.

C++

```
int numbers[5] = {1, 2, 3, 4, 5};

int *ptr = numbers; // "ptr" now points to
numbers[0]
```

Pointer Arithmetic

You can perform arithmetic operations (addition and subtraction) on pointers. This is particularly useful for traversing arrays.

Incrementing a Pointer: Moves the pointer to the next element in the array.

C++

```
ptr++; // "ptr" now points to numbers[1]
```

Decrementing a Pointer: Moves the pointer to the previous element.

C++

```
ptr--; // "ptr" now points back to numbers[0]
```

Adding an Integer: Moves the pointer forward by a specified number of elements.

C++

```
ptr += 2; // "ptr" now points to numbers[2]
```

Subtracting an Integer: Moves the pointer backward.

C++

```
ptr -= 1; // "ptr" now points to numbers[1]
```

Traversing Arrays with Pointers

You can use pointer arithmetic to iterate through an array and access its elements:

C++

```
for (int i = 0; i < 5; i++) {

    std::cout << *(ptr + i) << " "; // Print the
value at the current pointer location

}
```

This code will print: 1 2 3 4 5

Dynamic Memory Allocation

Pointers are essential for working with dynamic memory. Dynamic memory is allocated during program execution using the new operator. This allows you to create arrays whose size is not known at compile time.

C++

```cpp
int size;

std::cout << "Enter the size of the array: ";

std::cin >> size;


int *dynamicArray = new int[size]; // Allocate an array of the given size


// ... use the dynamicArray


delete[] dynamicArray; // Deallocate the memory when you're done
```

The delete[] operator is crucial for releasing the dynamically allocated memory back to the system when you're finished using it. Failing to do so can lead to memory leaks.

Benefits of Using Pointers with Arrays

Efficiency: Pointer arithmetic can be faster than using array indexing (`numbers[i]`).

Flexibility: Pointers allow you to work with dynamically allocated arrays.

Advanced Data Structures: Pointers are essential for building more complex data structures like linked lists and trees.

Example: Reversing an Array

C++

```cpp
#include <iostream>


void reverseArray(int *arr, int size) {

  int *start = arr;

  int *end = arr + size - 1;


  while (start < end) {

    int temp = *start;

    *start = *end;

    *end = temp;

    start++;

    end--;

  }
```

```cpp
}


int main() {

  int numbers[] = {1, 2, 3, 4, 5};

        int    size    =    sizeof(numbers)    /
sizeof(numbers[0]);


  std::cout << "Original array: ";

  for (int i = 0; i < size; i++) {

    std::cout << numbers[i] << " ";

  }


  reverseArray(numbers, size);


  std::cout << "\nReversed array: ";

  for (int i = 0; i < size; i++) {

    std::cout << numbers[i] << " ";

  }


  return 0;

}
```

This program demonstrates how to reverse an array using pointer arithmetic. The `reverseArray` function takes a pointer to the array and its size, and then uses two pointers (`start` and `end`) to swap elements from the beginning and end until they meet in the middle.

By mastering pointer arithmetic and dynamic memory allocation, you can write more efficient and flexible C++ programs that can handle data of varying sizes and structures.

5.3 Pointers and Functions: Passing by Reference

In C++, you can pass arguments to functions in two main ways: by value and by reference. Passing by reference using pointers allows functions to directly modify the original arguments passed to them, which can be very useful in certain situations.

Passing by Value (The Default)

By default, when you pass an argument to a function, C++ creates a copy of the argument's value and gives that copy to the function. Any changes the function makes to the parameter affect only the copy, not the original argument.

C++

```cpp
void increment(int num) {

  num++; // Increments the copy of "num"

}
```

```cpp
int main() {

    int x = 5;

    increment(x); // Pass "x" by value

    std::cout << x; // Output: 5 (x remains
unchanged)

    return 0;

}
```

Passing by Reference (Using Pointers)

To allow a function to modify the original argument, you pass the argument by reference using pointers. This gives the function access to the memory address of the argument.

C++

```cpp
void increment(int *numPtr) {

    (*numPtr)++; // Increments the value at the
address pointed to by "numPtr"

}


int main() {

    int x = 5;

    increment(&x); // Pass the address of "x"

    std::cout << x; // Output: 6 (x is modified)
```

```
    return 0;

}
```

In this example, `increment` receives a pointer to `x`. By dereferencing the pointer (`*numPtr`), the function can access and modify the original value of `x`.

Why Pass by Reference?

Modifying Arguments: When you need a function to modify the original values of the arguments passed to it.

Efficiency: Passing large data structures by reference avoids the overhead of copying them.

Returning Multiple Values: A function can modify multiple variables passed by reference, effectively returning multiple values.

Example: Swapping Values (Revisited)

Here's the `swap` function from the previous section, demonstrating passing by reference:

C++

```
void swap(int *a, int *b) {

    int temp = *a;

    *a = *b;

    *b = temp;

}
```

This function takes pointers to two integers, allowing it to swap their values by directly accessing their memory locations.

Important Notes

When passing by reference, make sure the function handles the pointers carefully to avoid modifying memory locations unintentionally.

C++ also offers another way to pass by reference using references (&). This provides similar functionality with a slightly different syntax, which you'll learn about later.

By understanding how to pass arguments by reference using pointers, you can write more versatile and efficient C++ functions that can manipulate data directly. This is a powerful technique that opens up new possibilities for your programs.

Chapter 6

Object-Oriented Programming (OOP) with C++

6.1 Classes and Objects: Encapsulation and Data Hiding

Object-oriented programming (OOP) is a powerful programming paradigm that allows you to model real-world entities as software objects. These objects have properties (data) and behaviors (functions), just like their real-world counterparts. Think of a "Car" object with properties like "color," "model," and "speed," and behaviors like "accelerate," "brake," and "turn."

Classes: The Blueprint

A class is like a blueprint or template for creating objects. It defines the structure and behavior of the objects that belong to it.

C++

```cpp
class Dog {

 public:

  std::string name;

  int age;


  void bark() {

   std::cout << "Woof!" << std::endl;
```

```
    }

};
```

This defines a class named `Dog` with:

Members: `name` (string) and `age` (integer) to store the dog's name and age.

Method: `bark()` to simulate the dog barking.

Objects: The Instances

An object is an instance of a class. It's like creating a specific dog from the blueprint.

C++

```
Dog myDog;    // Create an object named "myDog" of
type "Dog"
```

Encapsulation: Bundling Data and Methods

Encapsulation is one of the core principles of OOP. It means bundling the data (members) and the methods that operate on that data within a single unit (the class). This helps organize your code and makes it easier to manage.

Data Hiding: Protecting Data Integrity

Data hiding is another important aspect of encapsulation. It involves restricting access to the internal data of an object, preventing accidental or unintended modification from outside the class.

Access Specifiers: `public`, `private`, **and** `protected`

C++ provides access specifiers to control how members of a class can be accessed:

`public`: Members declared as `public` can be accessed from anywhere in your program.

`private`: Members declared as `private` can only be accessed from within the class itself (by its methods).

`protected`: (We'll discuss this in the next section on inheritance)

C++

```cpp
class Dog {

 private:

  int age;   // Now "age" is private


 public:

  std::string name;


  void bark() {

    std::cout << "Woof!" << std::endl;

  }


  void setAge(int newAge) { // A public method to set the age
```

```cpp
        if (newAge >= 0) {

            age = newAge;

        }

    }


    int getAge() { // A public method to get the
age

        return age;

    }

};
```

In this example, `age` is now private, so you cannot directly access it from outside the class (e.g., `myDog.age = 5;` would be an error). Instead, you use the public methods `setAge()` and `getAge()` to control how the age is modified and accessed.

Benefits of Encapsulation and Data Hiding

Data Protection: Prevents accidental corruption of data.

Code Maintainability: Changes to the internal implementation of a class are less likely to affect other parts of the program.

Modularity: Promotes code reusability and easier debugging.

By understanding classes, objects, encapsulation, and data hiding, you're well on your way to mastering object-oriented programming in C++. These concepts are fundamental to building robust and maintainable software.

6.2 Inheritance: Building Relationships

Inheritance is one of the most powerful features of object-oriented programming. It allows you to create new classes (derived classes) that inherit properties and behaviors from existing classes (base classes). This promotes code reusability and helps model real-world relationships.

Base Class (Parent Class)

The base class is the existing class that provides the foundation for the derived class. It defines common attributes and behaviors that can be shared by multiple derived classes.

Derived Class (Child Class)

The derived class inherits from the base class. It automatically gets all the public and protected members of the base class and can add its own unique members or modify inherited behaviors.

Example:

C++

```cpp
class Animal { // Base class

 public:

  std::string name;


  void eat() {

    std::cout << "The animal is eating." << std::endl;

  }
```

```cpp
};


class Dog : public Animal { // Derived class

  public:

   void bark() {

     std::cout << "Woof!" << std::endl;

   }

};
```

In this example, `Animal` is the base class, and `Dog` is the derived class. `Dog` inherits the `name` member and the `eat()` method from `Animal` and adds its own `bark()` method.

Creating Objects of Derived Classes

C++

```cpp
Dog myDog;

myDog.name = "Buddy";

myDog.eat();   // Inherited from Animal

myDog.bark();
```

Polymorphism: "Many Forms"

Polymorphism allows you to treat objects of different classes in a uniform way. This is particularly useful when dealing with a collection of objects of related types.

Example:

C++

```
Animal* animalPtr = &myDog; //  A pointer to the
base class can point to a derived class object

animalPtr->eat();  // Calls the eat() method of
the Dog class
```

Even though `animalPtr` is a pointer to `Animal`, it can point to a `Dog` object. When you call `eat()`, the correct version for the `Dog` class is executed. This is polymorphism in action!

Benefits of Inheritance

Code Reusability: Avoids code duplication by inheriting existing functionality.

Extensibility: Easily create new classes with specialized behaviors.

Maintainability: Changes to the base class automatically propagate to the derived classes.

Polymorphism: Enables flexible and dynamic code that can work with objects of different types.

Important Notes

`protected` **Access Specifier:** Members declared as `protected` in the base class are accessible to both the base class and its derived classes, but not from outside.

Types of Inheritance: C++ supports different types of inheritance, such as single inheritance (one base class), multiple inheritance (multiple base classes), and multilevel inheritance (a hierarchy of classes).

Inheritance is a cornerstone of object-oriented programming. By understanding how to create and use inheritance relationships, you can write more organized, reusable, and powerful C++ code.

6.3 Encapsulation and Abstraction: Access Specifiers and Information Hiding

Encapsulation and abstraction are closely related concepts in object-oriented programming that work together to create well-structured, maintainable, and robust code. They both involve hiding complexity and protecting data, but they achieve this in slightly different ways.

Encapsulation: Bundling Data and Methods

Encapsulation, as we discussed earlier, is the bundling of data (members) and the methods that operate on that data within a single unit (the class). This is like creating a capsule that contains both the data and the instructions for how to use it.

Abstraction: Showing Only the Essentials

Abstraction takes this concept further by hiding the internal details of how the class works and presenting only the essential information to the outside world. It's like providing a simplified interface to a complex system, allowing users to interact with it without needing to understand all the underlying mechanisms.

Access Specifiers: Controlling Access

Access specifiers (`public`, `private`, and `protected`) play a crucial role in both encapsulation and abstraction. They determine which parts of a class are visible and accessible from outside the class.

`public`: Members declared as `public` form the public interface of the class. They are the "essential information" that is exposed to the outside world.

`private`: Members declared as `private` are hidden from the outside world. They are the internal implementation details that are not relevant to users of the class.

`protected`: Members declared as `protected` are similar to `private` members, but they are also accessible to derived classes (we'll revisit this in the context of inheritance).

Information Hiding: Protecting Data Integrity

Information hiding is a key principle in both encapsulation and abstraction. It involves restricting access to the internal data of an object, preventing accidental or unintended modification from outside the class. This is achieved through the use of `private` and `protected` access specifiers.

Example:

C++

```
class Car {

  private:

    int fuelLevel;  // Hidden from the outside
```

```cpp
public:

  void accelerate() {

      // ... code to accelerate the car, which
might involve using fuelLevel

  }


  void refuel(int amount) {

      // ... code to add fuel, ensuring fuelLevel
doesn't exceed the maximum

  }


  int getFuelLevel() {

    return fuelLevel;

  }
};
```

In this example, the `fuelLevel` is a private member, hidden from the outside. You cannot directly access or modify it from outside the class. Instead, you use public methods like `accelerate()`, `refuel()`, and `getFuelLevel()` to interact with the car object in a controlled way.

Benefits of Encapsulation and Abstraction

Reduced Complexity: By hiding unnecessary details, abstraction simplifies the interaction with complex systems.

Increased Maintainability: Changes to the internal implementation of a class are less likely to affect other parts of the program.

Improved Code Reusability: Well-encapsulated classes can be easily reused in different parts of a program or even in other programs.

Enhanced Security: Information hiding protects data from unauthorized access and modification.

Encapsulation and abstraction are essential principles in object-oriented programming. By applying these principles effectively, you can create well-structured, maintainable, and robust C++ programs.

Chapter 7

Memory Management in C++

7.1 The Stack and the Heap: Automatic vs. Dynamic Memory Allocation

In C++, memory is divided into two main regions: the stack and the heap. Understanding how these regions work is crucial for managing memory effectively and preventing issues like memory leaks.

The Stack: Automatic Memory Allocation

The stack is a region of memory that operates in a Last-In, First-Out (LIFO) manner, like a stack of plates. It's used for **automatic memory allocation**, which means memory is allocated and deallocated automatically by the compiler.

How the Stack Works

When you declare a local variable inside a function, memory is allocated for that variable on the stack.

When the function ends, the memory for those variables is automatically deallocated (popped off the stack).

The stack is efficient and fast because memory allocation and deallocation are simple operations.

Example:

C++

```
void myFunction() {
```

```cpp
  int x = 10; // Memory for x is allocated on the
stack

  // ...

} // Memory for x is automatically deallocated
when the function ends
```

Limitations of the Stack

Limited Size: The stack has a fixed size, which can lead to stack overflow errors if you try to allocate too much memory.

Temporary Storage: Variables on the stack have a limited lifetime (within the function they are declared).

The Heap: Dynamic Memory Allocation

The heap is a larger region of memory used for **dynamic memory allocation**. This means you can allocate and deallocate memory manually during program execution.

How the Heap Works

You use the `new` operator to allocate memory on the heap.

You use the `delete` operator to deallocate memory when you're done with it.

The heap is more flexible than the stack because you have direct control over memory management.

Example:

C++

```cpp
int* ptr = new int; // Allocate memory for an
integer on the heap
```

```
*ptr = 20;

// ...

delete ptr; // Deallocate the memory
```

Benefits of the Heap

Flexible Size: The heap can grow as needed, limited only by the available system memory.

Persistent Storage: Data allocated on the heap can persist beyond the lifetime of a function.

Challenges of the Heap

Manual Management: You are responsible for deallocating memory using `delete` to prevent memory leaks.

Fragmentation: Over time, the heap can become fragmented, making it less efficient.

When to Use Each

Stack: Use the stack for local variables and temporary data within functions.

Heap: Use the heap for data that needs to persist beyond the lifetime of a function or for large data structures.

Example: Dynamic Array (Revisited)

C++

```
int size;

std::cout << "Enter the size of the array: ";

std::cin >> size;
```

```
int* dynamicArray = new int[size]; // Allocate an
array on the heap


// ... use the dynamicArray


delete[] dynamicArray; // Deallocate the array
```

This example shows how to allocate an array of a size determined at runtime using the heap.

By understanding the stack and the heap, and the differences between automatic and dynamic memory allocation, you can manage memory effectively in your C++ programs and prevent common memory-related issues.

7.2 `new` and `delete`: Allocating and Deallocating Memory

As we explored in the previous section, dynamic memory allocation allows you to allocate memory on the heap during program execution. This is essential for creating data structures whose size is not known at compile time or for data that needs to persist beyond the lifetime of a function.

The `new` Operator: Allocating Memory

The `new` operator allocates a block of memory of the specified type and returns a pointer to that memory location.

C++

```cpp
int* ptr = new int;     // Allocate memory for an integer

double* dPtr = new double; // Allocate memory for a double
```

You can also allocate memory for arrays using `new`:

C++

```cpp
int* arr = new int[10]; // Allocate memory for an array of 10 integers
```

Initializing Dynamically Allocated Memory

You can initialize dynamically allocated memory using parentheses `()` or curly braces `{}`:

C++

```cpp
int* ptr = new int(5);       // Initialize the integer to 5

double* dPtr = new double{3.14}; // Initialize the double to 3.14
```

The `delete` Operator: Deallocating Memory

When you're finished using dynamically allocated memory, it's crucial to deallocate it using the `delete` operator. This releases the memory back to the system, preventing memory leaks.

C++

```
delete ptr;      // Deallocate the memory pointed
to by "ptr"

delete dPtr; // Deallocate the memory pointed to
by "dPtr"
```

For arrays allocated with `new[]`, use `delete[]`:

C++

```
delete[] arr; // Deallocate the array
```

Importance of `delete`

Failing to deallocate memory using `delete` can lead to memory leaks. A memory leak occurs when your program allocates memory but doesn't release it, eventually consuming all available memory and causing your program to crash or become unstable.

Example: Creating a Dynamic String

C++

```
#include <iostream>

#include <string>


int main() {

    std::string* strPtr = new std::string; //
Allocate memory for a string on the heap
```

```cpp
    std::cout << "Enter a string: ";

    std::getline(std::cin, *strPtr); // Read input
into the dynamically allocated string


    std::cout << "You entered: " << *strPtr <<
std::endl;


    delete strPtr; // Deallocate the string


    return 0;

}
```

This example demonstrates how to dynamically allocate a string on the heap, read input into it, and then deallocate it.

Best Practices for `new` **and** `delete`

Always pair `new` **and** `delete`: For every `new` operation, there should be a corresponding `delete` operation.

Handle exceptions: Use exception handling (`try-catch` blocks) to ensure that `delete` is called even if errors occur.

Consider smart pointers: Smart pointers (which we'll discuss later) can help automate memory management and prevent memory leaks.

By understanding how to use `new` and `delete` effectively, you can manage dynamic memory in your C++ programs, creating flexible and efficient applications while avoiding the pitfalls of memory leaks.

7.3 Preventing Memory Leaks: Best Practices and Common Pitfalls

Memory leaks are a common problem in C++ programming, especially when dealing with dynamic memory allocation. They occur when your program allocates memory on the heap but fails to deallocate it when it's no longer needed. This can lead to your program consuming more and more memory over time, eventually causing it to crash or become unstable.

Best Practices for Preventing Memory Leaks

1 Pair `new` **and** `delete`: The most fundamental rule is to always pair every `new` operation with a corresponding `delete` operation. This ensures that every block of memory you allocate is eventually released back to the system.

2 Use RAII (Resource Acquisition Is Initialization): This idiom involves encapsulating dynamically allocated resources within objects. The resource is acquired when the object is constructed and released when the object is destructed. This ensures that resources are automatically released, even if exceptions occur.

3 Employ Smart Pointers: Smart pointers (e.g., `std::unique_ptr`, `std::shared_ptr`) are classes that manage dynamically allocated memory automatically. They release the memory when the smart pointer goes out of scope, preventing memory leaks.

4 Handle Exceptions Carefully: When using `new` and `delete` in code that might throw exceptions, use `try-catch` blocks to ensure that `delete` is called even if an exception occurs.

5 Avoid Raw Pointers When Possible: Minimize the use of raw pointers (`int*`, `double*`, etc.) and prefer smart pointers or other safer alternatives.

6 Minimize Global Variables: Global variables have a long lifetime and can easily lead to memory leaks if they point to dynamically allocated memory that is not properly deallocated.

7 Be Mindful of Circular References: Circular references occur when two or more objects hold pointers to each other, preventing them from being deallocated. Break these cycles by using weak pointers (`std::weak_ptr`) or other techniques.

8 Use Memory Debugging Tools: Tools like Valgrind, AddressSanitizer, and memory profilers can help detect memory leaks and other memory errors in your code.

Common Pitfalls that Lead to Memory Leaks

Forgetting to `delete`: The most common pitfall is simply forgetting to call `delete` after allocating memory with `new`.

Incorrect `delete`: Using `delete` instead of `delete[]` to deallocate arrays, or vice versa.

Exceptions: Exceptions can disrupt the normal flow of execution, potentially skipping `delete` calls.

Returning Raw Pointers: Returning a raw pointer to dynamically allocated memory from a function can lead to memory leaks if the caller forgets to `delete` it.

Hidden new **Calls:** Be aware of library functions or classes that might perform dynamic memory allocation internally. Make sure you understand their memory management requirements.

Example: Using Smart Pointers

C++

```cpp
#include <iostream>

#include <memory>


int main() {

    std::unique_ptr<int> ptr(new int(10)); // Create a unique pointer


  // Use the pointer

  std::cout << *ptr << std::endl;


    // No need to call delete, the memory is automatically deallocated

  // when "ptr" goes out of scope


  return 0;

}
```

In this example, `std::unique_ptr` automatically manages the memory for the integer. When `ptr` goes out of scope, the memory is automatically deallocated.

By following these best practices and being aware of common pitfalls, you can significantly reduce the risk of memory leaks in your C++ programs, leading to more stable and reliable applications.

Chapter 8

File Handling

8.1 Reading and Writing Text Files

Files are essential for storing and retrieving data persistently. In this section, we'll explore how to read and write text files in C++ using streams and file I/O operations.

Streams: The Flow of Data

In C++, streams are objects that represent the flow of data. They can be connected to various sources and destinations, such as the console, files, or network connections.

File I/O: `ofstream` and `ifstream`

For working with files, C++ provides two main stream classes:

`ofstream`: Used for writing data to files (output file stream).

`ifstream`: Used for reading data from files (input file stream).

Writing to a File

1 Include Header: `#include <fstream>`

Create an `ofstream` Object:

C++

```
std::ofstream    outputFile("myFile.txt");    //
Creates or overwrites a file named "myFile.txt"
```

Check for Errors:

C++

```cpp
if (outputFile.is_open()) {

    // ... file opened successfully

} else {

        std::cerr << "Error opening file!" << std::endl;

}
```

Write Data to the File:

C++

```cpp
outputFile << "This is some text." << std::endl;

outputFile << "Another line of text." << std::endl;
```

Close the File:

C++

```
outputFile.close();
```

Reading from a File

Include Header: `#include <fstream>`

Create an `ifstream` **Object:**

C++

```
std::ifstream inputFile("myFile.txt");
```

Check for Errors:

C++

```
if (inputFile.is_open()) {
    // ... file opened successfully
} else {
    std::cerr << "Error opening file!" << std::endl;
}
```

Read Data from the File:

C++

```cpp
std::string line;

while (std::getline(inputFile, line)) {

    std::cout << line << std::endl;

}
```

Close the File:

C++

```cpp
inputFile.close();
```

File Modes

You can specify different file modes when opening a file:

`ios::out`: For writing (default for `ofstream`).

`ios::app`: For appending to the end of the file.

`ios::in`: For reading (default for `ifstream`).

`ios::trunc`: Truncates the file to zero length if it exists (default for `ofstream`).

Example: Copying a File

C++

```cpp
#include <iostream>
#include <fstream>

int main() {
  std::ifstream sourceFile("source.txt");

  std::ofstream destinationFile("destination.txt");

  if (sourceFile.is_open() && destinationFile.is_open()) {

    std::string line;

    while (std::getline(sourceFile, line)) {

      destinationFile << line << std::endl;

    }

    std::cout << "File copied successfully!" << std::endl;

  } else {

    std::cerr << "Error opening files!" << std::endl;

  }
```

```
sourceFile.close();

destinationFile.close();


return 0;

}
```

This program copies the contents of "source.txt" to "destination.txt".

By understanding streams and file I/O operations, you can read and write text files in C++, enabling your programs to store and retrieve data persistently. This opens up a wide range of possibilities for your applications, from simple configuration files to complex data analysis.

8.2 Working with Binary Files: Data Serialization and Object Persistence

While text files are great for storing human-readable data, binary files offer a more efficient way to store data in its raw format. This is particularly useful for storing complex data structures, images, audio, and other non-textual information.

Binary Files: Raw Data

Binary files store data as a sequence of bytes, without any specific encoding or formatting. This makes them more compact and faster to read and write compared to text files.

Data Serialization: Converting Objects to Bytes

Data serialization is the process of converting complex data structures, like objects, into a stream of bytes that can be stored in a binary file. This allows you to save the state of your objects and later reconstruct them by reading the data back from the file.

Object Persistence: Saving and Loading Objects

Object persistence refers to the ability to save the state of objects to a persistent storage medium (like a file) and later reload them into memory, preserving their data and relationships.

Writing to a Binary File

Include Header: `#include <fstream>`

Create an `ofstream` **Object in Binary Mode:**

C++

```cpp
std::ofstream                outputFile("myData.bin",
std::ios::binary);
```

Write Data Using `write()`:

C++

```cpp
int age = 30;

outputFile.write(reinterpret_cast<char*>(&age),
sizeof(age));
```

Close the File:

C++

```
outputFile.close();
```

Reading from a Binary File

Include Header: `#include <fstream>`

Create an `ifstream` Object in Binary Mode:

C++

```
std::ifstream              inputFile("myData.bin",
std::ios::binary);
```

Read Data Using `read()`:

C++

```
int age;

inputFile.read(reinterpret_cast<char*>(&age),
sizeof(age));
```

Close the File:

C++

```
inputFile.close();
```

Example: Saving and Loading a Structure

C++

```cpp
#include <iostream>
#include <fstream>

struct Person {
    std::string name;
    int age;
};

int main() {
    // Save a Person object to a binary file
    Person person1 = {"Alice", 25};
```

```cpp
    std::ofstream    outputFile("person.bin",
std::ios::binary);

outputFile.write(reinterpret_cast<char*>(&person1
), sizeof(Person));

  outputFile.close();


  // Load the Person object from the binary file

  Person person2;

    std::ifstream    inputFile("person.bin",
std::ios::binary);

inputFile.read(reinterpret_cast<char*>(&person2),
sizeof(Person));

  inputFile.close();


  std::cout << "Name: " << person2.name << ",
Age: " << person2.age << std::endl;


  return 0;

}
```

This program demonstrates how to serialize a `Person` object to a binary file and then deserialize it back into memory.

Important Considerations

Endianness: Be aware of endianness (byte order) when reading and writing binary data across different systems.

Data Structures: For complex data structures, you might need to implement custom serialization and deserialization logic.

Error Handling: Always check for errors when opening and working with binary files.

By mastering binary file handling and data serialization, you can efficiently store and retrieve complex data in your C++ programs, enabling object persistence and a wide range of data-intensive applications.

8.3 Error Handling and File Management

When working with files, things don't always go as planned. Files might not exist, you might not have the necessary permissions, or the disk could be full. Robust file handling requires effective error handling to gracefully handle these situations.

Exception Handling: Catching and Handling Errors

C++ provides a mechanism called exception handling to deal with runtime errors. Exceptions are objects that are "thrown" when an error occurs. You can "catch" these exceptions and handle them appropriately.

try-catch **Blocks**

The try-catch block is the core of exception handling:

C++

```
try {
  // Code that might throw an exception
```

```cpp
} catch (const std::exception& e) {

  // Code to handle the exception

    std::cerr << "Error: " << e.what() <<
std::endl;

}
```

try **block:** Contains the code that might throw an exception.

catch **block:** Handles exceptions of the specified type.

Example: Handling File Opening Errors

C++

```cpp
#include <iostream>

#include <fstream>


int main() {

  try {


                              std::ifstream
inputFile("nonexistent_file.txt");

    if (!inputFile.is_open()) {

      throw std::runtime_error("Could not open
file.");

    }

    // ... process the file
```

```cpp
        inputFile.close();

    } catch (const std::runtime_error& e) {

        std::cerr << "Error: " << e.what() <<
std::endl;

    }


    return 0;

}
```

This code throws a `std::runtime_error` if the file cannot be opened. The `catch` block then catches this exception and prints an error message.

File System Interaction

C++ provides functions for interacting with the file system, such as:

Checking if a file exists:

C++

```cpp
#include <filesystem> // C++17 or later


if (std::filesystem::exists("myFile.txt")) {

    // ... file exists

}
```

Creating directories:

C++

```cpp
std::filesystem::create_directory("myDirectory");
```

Deleting files:

C++

```cpp
std::filesystem::remove("myFile.txt");
```

Renaming files:

C++

```cpp
std::filesystem::rename("oldName.txt",
"newName.txt");
```

Getting file size:

C++

```
std::uintmax_t                    fileSize         =
std::filesystem::file_size("myFile.txt");
```

Error Handling with File System Operations

It's important to handle potential errors when performing file system operations. For example, you might try to create a directory that already exists or delete a file that is in use.

C++

```
try {

std::filesystem::create_directory("myDirectory");

} catch (const std::filesystem::filesystem_error& e) {

    std::cerr << "Error creating directory: " << e.what() << std::endl;

}
```

Best Practices

Handle exceptions: Use `try-catch` blocks to handle potential errors during file operations.

Check return values: Many file system functions return values indicating success or failure. Always check these values.

Use appropriate error messages: Provide informative error messages to the user.

Close files properly: Ensure that files are closed using `close()` when you're finished with them.

Consider using libraries: Libraries like Boost.Filesystem can provide more advanced file system functionality and error handling.

By combining exception handling with file system interaction, you can create robust and reliable C++ programs that can gracefully handle errors and interact with the file system effectively.

Chapter 9

Advanced C++ Concepts

9.1 Templates: Generic Programming

Imagine you need to write a function to find the maximum of two numbers. You could write separate functions for integers, doubles, and other data types. But what if there was a way to write a single function that could work with any data type? That's where templates come in!

Templates: The Blueprint for Code

Templates allow you to write generic code that can work with different data types without being rewritten for each one. They're like blueprints that the compiler uses to generate specific versions of your code based on the types you provide.

Function Templates

A function template defines a generic function that can operate on various data types.

C++

```cpp
template <typename T>

T maximum(T a, T b) {

  return (a > b) ? a : b;

}
```

template <typename T>: This declares a template parameter T, which can represent any data type.

T maximum(T a, T b): The function takes two arguments of type T and returns a value of type T.

Using Function Templates

You can use a function template by providing the specific data type you want to use:

C++

```cpp
int maxInt = maximum(5, 10);          // Uses maximum<int>

double maxDouble = maximum(3.14, 2.71); // Uses maximum<double>
```

The compiler automatically generates the appropriate versions of the maximum function for int and double.

Class Templates

You can also create class templates, which define generic classes that can work with different data types.

C++

```cpp
template <typename T>

class MyArray {

 private:

  T* data;

  int size;
```

```cpp
public:

  // ... constructors, methods, etc.

};
```

This defines a generic `MyArray` class that can hold elements of any data type `T`.

Using Class Templates

C++

```cpp
MyArray<int> intArray(10);   // Creates an array
of integers

MyArray<double> doubleArray(5); // Creates an
array of doubles
```

Benefits of Templates

Code Reusability: Write code once and use it with different data types.

Flexibility: Create adaptable code that can work with various data structures.

Type Safety: Templates provide compile-time type checking, ensuring that the code is used with compatible types.

Efficiency: Template-based code is generated at compile time, resulting in efficient and optimized code without runtime overhead.

Example: A Generic Stack Class

C++

```cpp
#include <iostream>

template <typename T>
class Stack {
 private:
  T* data;
  int top;
  int capacity;

 public:
    Stack(int    capacity)    :    top(-1),
capacity(capacity) {
    data = new T[capacity];
  }

  ~Stack() {
    delete[] data;
  }
```

```cpp
  void push(const T& item) {

    if (top < capacity - 1) {

      data[++top] = item;

    } else {

      // Handle stack overflow

    }

  }


  T pop() {

    if (top >= 0) {

      return data[top--];

    } else {

      // Handle stack underflow

    }

  }
};


int main() {

  Stack<int> intStack(5);

  intStack.push(10);
```

```cpp
    intStack.push(20);


    Stack<std::string> stringStack(3);

    stringStack.push("Hello");

    stringStack.push("World");


    return 0;

}
```

This example demonstrates a generic `Stack` class that can be used to create stacks of integers, strings, or any other data type.

Templates are a powerful tool for generic programming in C++. They enable you to write reusable, flexible, and efficient code that can work with a wide range of data types and data structures. By understanding how to use templates effectively, you can significantly improve the quality and maintainability of your C++ code.

9.2 Standard Template Library (STL): Containers, Algorithms, and Iterators

The Standard Template Library (STL) is a powerful part of C++ that provides a collection of ready-to-use data structures (containers) and algorithms that operate on them. It's like a toolbox filled with efficient and well-tested tools for common programming tasks, saving you the effort of reinventing the wheel.

Containers: Organizing Your Data

Containers are objects that store collections of elements. The STL offers a variety of containers to suit different needs:

Sequence Containers: Store elements in a linear order.

`std::vector`: Dynamic array that can grow or shrink as needed.

`std::list`: Doubly linked list that allows efficient insertion and deletion at any position.

`std::deque`: Double-ended queue that supports efficient insertion and deletion at both ends.

Associative Containers: Store elements in a sorted order, allowing efficient searching.

`std::set`: Stores unique elements in a sorted order.

`std::map`: Stores key-value pairs in a sorted order, allowing efficient lookup by key.

Unordered Associative Containers: Store elements in an unordered manner, using hash tables for efficient lookup.

`std::unordered_set`: Stores unique elements in an unordered manner.

`std::unordered_map`: Stores key-value pairs in an unordered manner.

Algorithms: Manipulating Your Data

Algorithms are functions that perform operations on containers. The STL provides a wide range of algorithms for tasks like:

Sorting: `std::sort, std::stable_sort`

Searching: `std::find`, `std::binary_search`

Modifying: `std::transform`, `std::replace`

Numeric: `std::accumulate`, `std::inner_product`

Iterators: Connecting Containers and Algorithms

Iterators are objects that act like pointers to elements within a container. They provide a generic way to access and traverse elements without exposing the internal structure of the container.

Types of Iterators:

Input iterators: For reading elements.

Output iterators: For writing elements.

Forward iterators: For reading and writing elements in a forward direction.

Bidirectional iterators: For reading and writing elements in both directions.

Random access iterators: For accessing elements directly using indexing.

Example: Sorting a Vector

C++

```cpp
#include <iostream>

#include <vector>

#include <algorithm>


int main() {

  std::vector<int> numbers = {5, 2, 8, 1, 9};
```

```cpp
    std::sort(numbers.begin(), numbers.end()); //
Sort the vector

    for (int number : numbers) {

      std::cout << number << " ";

    }

    std::cout << std::endl; // Output: 1 2 5 8 9


    return 0;

}
```

This example demonstrates how to use the `std::sort` algorithm to sort a vector of integers. `numbers.begin()` and `numbers.end()` return iterators that point to the beginning and end of the vector, respectively.

Benefits of Using the STL

Efficiency: STL components are highly optimized for performance.

Reusability: Use existing data structures and algorithms instead of writing your own.

Consistency: STL follows consistent conventions, making it easier to learn and use.

Extensibility: You can create your own containers and algorithms that work seamlessly with the STL.

The STL is a powerful tool for C++ programmers. By understanding how to use containers, algorithms, and iterators effectively, you can write more efficient, concise, and maintainable code. It's a valuable asset for any C++ developer to have in their toolbox.

9.3 Exception Handling: Dealing with Errors (`try`, `catch`, `throw`)

Errors are an inevitable part of programming. Whether it's invalid user input, a network connection failure, or a file not found, your program needs to be able to handle these situations gracefully. Exception handling provides a structured way to deal with errors in C++, preventing your program from crashing and allowing you to recover or provide informative error messages.

Exceptions: Signaling Errors

Exceptions are objects that signal that an exceptional situation or error has occurred. When an error occurs, you can "throw" an exception to indicate that something went wrong.

`try` Block: Monitoring for Exceptions

The `try` block encloses the code that might potentially throw an exception. It's like saying, "Try to execute this code, and if something goes wrong, I'll handle it."

C++

```
try {
```

```cpp
  // Code that might throw an exception
}
```

catch Block: Handling Exceptions

The catch block follows the try block and specifies how to handle exceptions of a particular type. It's like saying, "If an exception of this type is thrown, do this."

C++

```cpp
catch (const std::exception& e) {
  // Code to handle the exception
    std::cerr << "Error: " << e.what() << std::endl;
}
```

catch (const std::exception& e): This catches exceptions of type std::exception (or any type derived from it). The e object provides information about the exception.

throw Statement: Raising Exceptions

The throw statement is used to throw an exception when an error condition is encountered.

C++

```cpp
if (divisor == 0) {
  throw std::runtime_error("Division by zero!");
```

```
}
```

This code throws a `std::runtime_error` exception with the message "Division by zero!" if the `divisor` is zero.

Example: Handling Invalid Input

C++

```cpp
#include <iostream>


int main() {

  int age;


  try {

    std::cout << "Enter your age: ";

    std::cin >> age;


    if (age < 0) {

        throw std::invalid_argument("Age cannot be negative.");

    }


    // ... process the age
```

```cpp
    } catch (const std::invalid_argument& e) {

        std::cerr << "Error: " << e.what() <<
std::endl;

    }


    return 0;

}
```

This code throws an `std::invalid_argument` exception if the user enters a negative age. The `catch` block handles this exception and prints an error message.

Benefits of Exception Handling

Separation of Concerns: Separates error handling code from normal program logic.

Structured Error Handling: Provides a clear and organized way to handle errors.

Propagating Errors: Exceptions can propagate up the call stack until they are caught.

Preventing Crashes: Handles errors gracefully, preventing program crashes.

Best Practices

Throw exceptions for exceptional situations: Don't use exceptions for normal program flow.

Catch specific exceptions: Catch exceptions by their specific types to handle different errors appropriately.

Provide informative error messages: Include helpful information in exception messages.

Clean up resources: Use `finally` blocks or RAII to ensure resources are released even if exceptions occur.

Exception handling is a powerful mechanism for dealing with errors in C++. By understanding how to use `try`, `catch`, and `throw`, you can write robust and reliable programs that can handle unexpected situations effectively.

Chapter 10

Building Your First C++ Project

10.1 Choosing a Project Idea (Simple games, utilities, simulations)

Choosing a Project Idea

Congratulations! You've made it to the final chapter, where you'll put your newfound C++ skills to the test by building your first project. This is an exciting opportunity to apply what you've learned and create something you can be proud of.

But first, you need to choose a project idea. Here are some suggestions to get your creative juices flowing, categorized into simple games, utilities, and simulations:

Simple Games

Number Guessing Game: The computer generates a random number, and the player has to guess it within a certain number of tries.

Hangman: The player has to guess a hidden word by suggesting letters.

Tic-Tac-Toe: A classic two-player game where players take turns marking spaces on a grid.

Text-Based Adventure Game: Create a story-driven game where the player makes choices that affect the outcome.

Simple Card Game: Implement a basic card game like War or Go Fish.

Utilities

To-Do List Manager: A program to keep track of tasks and deadlines.

Simple Calculator: A basic calculator that performs arithmetic operations.

Unit Converter: Converts between different units of measurement (e.g., meters to feet, Celsius to Fahrenheit).

File Organizer: Organizes files in a directory based on type, date, or other criteria.

Password Generator: Generates strong and random passwords.

Simulations

Coin Toss Simulator: Simulates flipping a coin a certain number of times and displays the results.

Dice Rolling Simulator: Simulates rolling dice and displays the outcomes.

Simple Physics Simulation: Simulates a ball bouncing or a pendulum swinging.

Basic Ecosystem Simulation: Models a simple ecosystem with predators and prey.

Traffic Simulation: Simulates traffic flow on a road or intersection.

Tips for Choosing a Project

Start Simple: Choose a project that is challenging but achievable with your current skills.

Pick Something You're Interested In: You'll be more motivated to work on a project that you find interesting.

Break it Down: Divide the project into smaller, manageable tasks.

Don't Be Afraid to Experiment: This is a learning experience, so don't be afraid to try new things and make mistakes.

Have Fun! Enjoy the process of creating something with your own code.

Once you've chosen a project idea, it's time to move on to the next stage: planning and design.

10.2 Planning and Design

Now that you have a project idea in mind, it's time to roll up your sleeves and start planning! Just like an architect wouldn't build a skyscraper without blueprints, you shouldn't start coding without a plan. This stage involves breaking down your project into smaller parts and, if necessary, designing the classes you'll need.

Breaking Down the Problem

1 Define the Core Functionality: What is the main purpose of your project? What are the essential features it needs to have?

2 Identify the Inputs and Outputs: What kind of data will your program take as input? What kind of output will it produce?

3 Decompose into Modules: Break down the project into smaller, more manageable modules or components. Each module should have a specific responsibility.

4 Consider the Data Structures: What kind of data structures will you need to store and organize your data (e.g., arrays, vectors, maps)?

5 Outline the Algorithms: What algorithms will you need to implement to achieve the desired functionality (e.g., sorting, searching, calculations)?

Example: Planning a Number Guessing Game

Let's say you're building a number guessing game. Here's how you might break it down:

Core Functionality: The computer generates a random number, and the player has to guess it.

Inputs: Player's guesses.

Outputs: Messages to the player (e.g., "Too high!", "Too low!", "You win!").

Modules:

Random number generation.

Input validation (ensure the player enters a valid number).

Comparison of the guess with the secret number.

Keeping track of the number of guesses.

Displaying messages to the player.

Data Structures: You might not need complex data structures for this simple game.

Algorithms: You'll need an algorithm to generate random numbers within a range.

Designing Classes (If Applicable)

If your project involves object-oriented programming, you'll need to design the classes you'll use.

1 Identify Objects: What are the key entities or concepts in your project that can be represented as objects?

2 Define Class Responsibilities: What data should each class hold? What actions should each class be able to perform?

3 Determine Class Relationships: How do the classes relate to each other? Are there inheritance relationships or other associations?

4 Consider Encapsulation and Abstraction: How will you encapsulate data and provide a clear public interface for your classes?

Example: Designing Classes for a To-Do List Manager

Objects: `Task`, `TaskList`

`Task` **Class:**

Data: `description` (string), `dueDate` (date), `priority` (enum), `completed` (boolean).

Methods: `markAsComplete()`, `setDueDate()`, `setPriority()`, etc.

`TaskList` **Class:**

Data: A container (e.g., `std::vector`) to hold `Task` objects.

Methods: `addTask()`, `removeTask()`, `displayTasks()`, `sortByDueDate()`, etc.

Tools for Planning and Design

Flowcharts: Visualize the flow of your program's logic.

UML Diagrams: Model classes and their relationships.

Pseudocode: Write informal code-like descriptions of your algorithms.

By carefully planning and designing your project before you start coding, you'll have a clear roadmap to follow, making the development process smoother and more efficient. You'll also be less likely to encounter unexpected problems or have to rewrite large portions of your code later.

10.3 Implementation and Testing

With a solid plan in place, it's time for the most exciting part: bringing your project to life through code! This stage involves writing the actual C++ code, testing it thoroughly, and refining it until it meets your expectations.

Coding

1 Follow Your Plan: Use your plan and design as a guide, but be flexible and adapt as needed.

2 Write Clean Code: Use meaningful variable names, add comments, and follow consistent formatting to make your code readable and maintainable.

3 Start with Core Functionality: Focus on implementing the core features of your project first.

4 Break Down Complex Tasks: Divide complex tasks into smaller, more manageable functions or methods.

5 Test as You Go: Don't wait until you've written all the code to start testing. Test small portions of code as you write them.

Debugging

Debugging is the process of finding and fixing errors (bugs) in your code. It's an essential part of software development.

1 Use a Debugger: IDEs provide debuggers that allow you to step through your code line by line, inspect variables, and set breakpoints.

2 Print Debugging: Use `std::cout` to print values of variables or messages to track the flow of your program.

3 Analyze Error Messages: Pay close attention to compiler error messages and runtime errors. They often provide valuable clues about the source of the problem.

4 Test with Different Inputs: Try running your program with various inputs to uncover edge cases and unexpected behavior.

5 Isolate the Problem: If you have a complex bug, try to isolate the problematic part of your code by commenting out sections or writing smaller test programs.

Refinement

Once you have a working version of your project, it's time to refine it.

1 Improve Code Quality: Refactor your code to make it more efficient, readable, and maintainable.

2 Add Features: Add any additional features or enhancements that you initially planned or that you come up with during development.

3 Optimize Performance: If necessary, optimize your code for speed or memory usage.

4 Polish the User Interface: If your project has a user interface, make sure it's clear, intuitive, and user-friendly.

5 Get Feedback: Ask others to test your project and provide feedback.

Testing

Thorough testing is crucial to ensure that your project works correctly and meets its requirements.

1 Unit Testing: Test individual functions or methods in isolation.

2 Integration Testing: Test how different modules of your project work together.

3 System Testing: Test the entire system as a whole.

4 User Acceptance Testing (UAT): Have potential users test your project to ensure it meets their needs.

Example: Testing a Calculator

If you're building a calculator, you might write unit tests to verify that each arithmetic operation (+, −, *, /) produces the correct result. You would also perform integration tests to ensure that the calculator handles user input and output correctly. Finally, you would conduct system tests to make sure the calculator works as a whole, including error handling and any additional features.

By following a systematic approach to implementation, debugging, refinement, and testing, you can create high-quality C++ projects that are reliable, efficient, and user-friendly. Remember to celebrate your successes and learn from your mistakes along the way. Happy coding!